AVENGERS OF INDIA

SCOPE FOR THE FARMERS IN TOURISM

AF570317

ARSHAQ HABIB

Copyright © Arshaq Habib
All Rights Reserved.

ISBN 979-888629303-6

This book has been published with all efforts taken to make the material error-free after the consent of the author. However, the author and the publisher do not assume and hereby disclaim any liability to any party for any loss, damage, or disruption caused by errors or omissions, whether such errors or omissions result from negligence, accident, or any other cause.

While every effort has been made to avoid any mistake or omission, this publication is being sold on the condition and understanding that neither the author nor the publishers or printers would be liable in any manner to any person by reason of any mistake or omission in this publication or for any action taken or omitted to be taken or advice rendered or accepted on the basis of this work. For any defect in printing or binding the publishers will be liable only to replace the defective copy by another copy of this work then available.

Firstly I would like to thank my parents and family members for all the support. I am grateful to Dr. Wajeeda Bano, Economics Department and Dr. A M Khan for the encouragement. In particular I would like to thank my PhD supervisor Dr. Mustiary Begum at Mangalore University, Dr. Joseph PD, Coordinator of MBA (Tourism and Travel Management) Mangalore University, Prof Shekar Naik, Associate Professor of MBA (Tourism and Travel Management), Dr Jagath Thimmaiah, Principal of FMKMC college, Prof Mahadeviah, Coordinator of Tourism and travel management for all the support. I would like to thank my best friend Prof. Noushad H, Assistant Professor at Government First Grade College Mudigere. I wish to place my gratitude to my colleagues and students of Field Marshal KM Cariappa College who has contributed directly or indirectly in the making of this book. Sincere thanks to my sister Fathima Afreen for editing and correcting this book.Sincere thanks to Mrs. Sowmya SN. I would also like to thank Shameer SR for the guidance and the designing of this book.

Contents

Acknowledgements

Special Thanks to Jishma Rejina for designing the cover page.

CHAPTER ONE

ABSTRACT

AGRO-TOURISM: SCOPE AND OPPORTUNITIES FOR THE FARMERS IN SOUTH INDIA

Tourism is now well recognised as an engine of growth in the various economies in the world. Several countries have transformed their economies by developing their tourism potential. Tourism has great capacity to generate large-scale employment and additional income sources to the skilled and unskilled. Today the concept of traditional tourism has been changed. Some new areas of the tourism have been emerged like AgroTourism. Promotion of tourism would bring many direct and indirect benefits to the people. Agro-tourism is a way of sustainable tourist development and multi-activity in rural areas through which the visitor has the opportunity to get aware with agricultural areas, agricultural occupations, local products, traditional food and the daily life of the rural people, as well as the cultural elements and traditions. Moreover, this activity brings visitors closer to nature and rural activities in which they can participate, be entertained and feel the pleasure of touring. Agro-Tourism is helpful to the both farmers and urban peoples. It has provided an additional income source to the farmers and employment opportunity to the family members and rural youth. But, there are some problems in the process of the development of such centres. Hence, the government and other related authorities should try to support these activities in South Indian Region for the rural development and increase income level of the farmers. The farmers should also try to establish their co-operative society for the development of agro-tourism centres. The agro-tourism may become a cash crop for the farmers in South Indian Region and also an instrument of the rural employment generation.

CHAPTER TWO

INTRODUCTION

Tourism is now well recognised as an engine of growth in the various economies in the world. Several countries have transformed their economies by developing their tourism potential. Tourism has great capacity to generate large-scale employment and additional income sources to the skilled and unskilled. Today the concept of traditional tourism has been changed. Some new areas of the tourism have been emerged like AgroTourism. Promotion of tourism would bring many direct and indirect benefits to the people. Agro-tourism is an innovative agricultural activity related to tourism and agriculture both. It has a great capacity to create additional source of income and employment opportunities to the farmers. South India is one of the major tourist centres in the India and there is large scope and great potential to develop agro-tourism.

OBJECTIVES

The objectives of this paper are follows:

** To examine the importance of agro-tourism development in South India.*

** To define a suitable framework for the of agro- tourism centres in the view of marginal and small farmers.*

** To identify the problems of the agro-tourism and make suggestions to establishment and operations of agro-tourism.*

HYPOTHESES

The hypothesis of the study is- the agro-tourism is an additional co-activity for the farmers. It provides additional income source and employment opportunity to the farmers and rural peoples. It gives new look for the agri-business. There is need of such types of activities in the South India.

IMPORTANCE OF THE STUDY

Agriculture is the most important occupation in the India. But, today it becomes unprofitable due the irregular mansoon, prices fluctuations of Agro-products and some internal weaknesses of the agriculture sector.Hence, there is need to do some innovative activities in the agriculture, which will help to farmers, rural people. Urban population is increasing day by day in the South India, today the urban people's world is restricted in the closed door flats, offices, clubs, television, video games, spicy fast food, computer, internet, and so on. They can see nature only on television or screen of the computers. More over some people living in the cities do not have relatives in villages and they never visited or stayed in village. These people want to enjoy rural life but there is problem of such type of facilities. Hence, it is opportunity to the farmers for the development of the agro-tourism centres and it serves him and create additional income source.

SCOPE AND METHODOLOGY OF THE STUDY

The scope of the study is limited to examine the benefits and applicability of agrotourism business in South India. The study includes their benefits and problems. As well as it includes appropriate framework regarding to establish the agro-tourism centres in the South India. The present study was conducted on the agro-tourism is based on secondary data. The data has been furnished from the related articles, research papers, reports and 11th plan document of the government of India. Some data has been furnished from the websites of the government of India and South India, as well as ministry of agriculture. Some ideas have been taken from the Tourism Development Corporation of South India.

CHAPTER THREE

CONCEPT OF AGRO-TOURISM

A term 'Agro-Tourism' is a new face of tourism. An agro-tourism is farm based business that is open to the public. These specialized agro-tourism destinations generally offer things to see, things to do, and produce or gifts to buy, and are open to the public. Agritourism is defined as "Travel that combines agricultural or rural settings with products of agricultural operations – all within a tourism experience". Agro-Tourism is that Agri-Business activity, when a native farmers or person of the area offers tours to their agriculture farm to allow a person to view them growing, harvesting, and processing locally grown foods, such as coconuts, pineapple, sugar cane, corn, or any agriculture produce the person would notencounter in their city or home country. Often the farmers would provide a home-stay opportunity and education". Agro-Tourism and Eco-Tourism are closely related to each other. Eco-Tourism provided by the tour companies but, in the agro-tourism farmers offer tours to their agriculture farm and providing entertainment, education and fun-filled experiences for the urban people. Agro-tourism is a way of sustainable tourist development and multi-activity in rural areas through which the visitor has the opportunity to get aware with agricultural areas, agricultural occupations, local products, traditional food and the daily life of the rural people, as well as the cultural

elements and traditions. Moreover, this activity brings visitors closer to nature and rural activities in which they can participate, be entertained and feel the pleasure of touring.

WHO CAN START AGRIO-TOURISM CENTRES

The individual farmer can start agro-tourism who have minimum two hector land, farm house, water resource and is interested to entertain the tourists. Apart from the individual farmer, agricultural co-operatives institute, Non-Government organisations, Agricultural Universities, and agricultural colleges may start their centres. Even Grampanchayats can start such centres in their operational areas with the help of villagers and farmers.

REQUIREMENTS FOR AGRO-TOURISM CENTRES

Researcher has identified the minimum requirements for the agro-tourism centre.

To develop an agro-tourism in their farm, the farmer / farmers must have basic infrastructure and facilities in their farm as follows:

Infrastructure Facilities:

- *Accommodation facilities at same place or alliance with nearest hotels.*

• Farmhouse, which has the rural look and feel comfortable along with all minimum required facilities.

• Rich resources in agriculture namely water and plants at the place.

• Cooking equipments for cooking food, if tourists have interested.

• Emergency medical cares with first aid box.

• The well or lake or swimming tank for fishing, swimming

• Bullock cart, cattle shade, telephone facilities etc

• Goat farm, Emu (Ostrich bird) farm, sericulture farm, green house, etc.

Facilities Be Provided

• Offer authentic rural Indian food for breakfast, lunch and dinner.

• Farmers should offer to see and participate in the agricultural activities.

- *Offer an opportunity to participate in the rural games to the tourist*

- *Provide information them about the culture, dress, arts, crafts, festivals, rural traditions and also give possible demonstration of some arts.*

- *Offer bullock cart for riding and horse riding, buffalo ride in the water, fishing facility in your pounds or nearest lake.*

- *Offer fruits, corns, groundnuts, sugarcane and other agro-products as per availability.*

- *Show local birds, animals and waterfalls etc and give authentic information about them.*

- *Must provide safety to tourists with the support of alliance hospitals.*

- *Arrange folk dance programme, Shekoti folk songs bhajan, kirtana, lezim dance, dhangari gaja, etc.*

- *Make available some agro-product to purchase to the tourist*

- *Offer pollution free environment to the tourists*

• Try to create interest about the village culture for the future tourism business.

• Introduce the tourists with imminent persons of your village.

• Employ well-trained staff or funny (comedy) persons with good communication skill to entertain the tourist.

• To have authentic information regarding the railway and bus time table for the help of tourists.

Farmer can also provide other additional facilities to their requirements for the better satisfaction of tourists.

LOCATION FOR THE AGRO-TOURISM CENTRE

Location is most the important factor for success in the agro-tourism. The location of the centre must easy to arrive and have a good natural background. Urban tourists are interested into enjoying the nature and rural life. So, farmers should develop their centre in the rural areas only which have a beautiful natural background to attract urban tourist in your farm.The place of agro-tourism centre must be easy accessible by roads and railways. Tourists want to enjoy some historical and natural tourist places along with the agro-tourism. Hence, the centre should be developed near of these tourist places. It is more beneficial to both tourist and farmers.

BENEFITS OF AGRO-TOURISM CENTRES

Agro-Tourism has the potential to change the economic face of traditional agriculture. The benefits of agro-tourism development are manifold. It would bring many direct and indirect benefits to the farmers and rural people. Some of the benefits are following:-

? Employment opportunities to the farmers including farm family members and youth

? Additional income source for the farmers to protest against income fluctuation.

? Cultural transformation between urban and rural people including social moral values

? Farmers can improve their standard of living due to the contacts with urban people.

? Benefits to the urban people, they can understand about the rural life and know about the agricultural activities.

? It support for rural and agricultural development process.

? Help to the reduce burden on the other traditional tourist centres.

AGRO-TOURISM AND TRADITIONAL TOURISM

Agro-tourism also a tourism business but it is different from the traditional tourism because it has a base of agriculture and rural lifestyle. Generally tourism has provided to see and enjoy the natural places as well as some heritages. But, agro-tourism has a tourism with includes experience, education and cultural transformation. It varies special from general tourism in the following manner:

? It provides pollution and noise free sites for travel and tourism at rural background.

? The cost of food, accommodation, recreation and travel is minimum in agrotourism.

? Agro-tourism can satisfy the curiosity of urban peoples about sources of food, plants, animals, and industrial agro-raw materials.

? It provides information about the rural handicrafts, languages, culture, tradition, dresses and lifestyle.

? A family environment at the tourist place, is one of the most important characteristics in the agro-tourism.

? In the agro-tour, tourists not only see and watch agriculture farms but they can also participate in the agricultural activities and experience the farming.

? It provides natural situations for watching birds, animals, water bodies etc.

? Agro-tourism creates awareness about rural life and knowledge about agriculture.

It also provides opportunity for education through experience of farming and knowledge about the rural life including entertainment. Agro-tourism is an instrument of urban-rural connectivity through the tours.

WHY TO PROMOTE AGRO-TOURISM IN SOUTH INDIA

Agriculture business is becoming more unsecured in South India due to the irregular mansoon, unsecured product prices. Many farmers cannot afford it and have a 8 problem of indebtedness. Due to the agricultural problems some farmers are committing to suicide in various districts of the South India. More than 1,50,000 farmers committed suicide between 1997 and 2005 in the India. Hence, there is need of start any of allied agri-business to support their farming and create allied income source from farm. In order to encourage farmers to establish small and viable agro-business activity, like agro-tourism. It offers several potential benefits to farm operators. It can help supplement income generation activity while providing an opportunity to more fully employ assets, including farm household members. South India has a great potential of agro-tourism due to the beautiful natural site and basic infrastructures.

CHAPTER FOUR

AGRO-TOURISM POTENTIAL IN SOUTH INDIA

South India has both in larg areas and population. Nestled in the Western Ghats and the Sahyadri mountain ranges have several hill stations and water reservoirs with semi-evergreen and deciduous forests. There are many tourist centres in South India which are the supporting natural environment for the agrotourism centres in South India. Principal crops include rice, Jowar, Bajra, wheat, pulses, turmeric, onions, cotton, sugarcane and several oil seeds including groundnut, sunflower and soyabean. The state has huge areas, under fruit cultivation of which mangoes, bananas, grapes, and oranges etc. South India is blessed with a rich and diversified cultural heritage. The state has several communities belonging to different religions, and a number of festivities colours the culture of South India with the spirit of exuberance. Other than nature and culture there is an enough road and rail connectivity in urban rural areas to travel in rural South India. South India abounds in numerous tourist attractions ranging from ancient cave temples, unspoiled beaches, ancient forts and monuments, forests and wildlife, unique hill stations, pilgrimage, centres, and a rich tradition of festivals, art and culture. Thus all the districts in South India have a tourism potential. Some

following notable factors are helpful to the agro-tourism in South India.

· Tourist places are already exist to support Agro-Tourism · Good communication and transport facilities · Green house cultivation of long stem cut flowers, vegetables, fruits etc.

· State has 13 lakh hectares area under horticulture South India now is a major horticulture state.

· South India is already established as one of the top tourist destination in the world

· South India is major producer of fruit, spices, medicinal and aromatic plant allowed under horticulture in India.

· There are an increasing number of tourists preferring non-urban tourist spots.

· South India has diverse Agro-climatic conditions, diverse crops, people, deserts, mountains, which provide scope for promotion of all season, multi-location agrotourism

Culture of South India is very glorious with a great variety. It gives a unique identity to the rural South India.

SUPPORTS TO THE AGRO-TOURISM IN SOUTH INDIA

Promotion of Agro-Tourism involves some more important stakeholders namely Ministry of Agriculture and rural development ministry of the state and central governments. To promote domestic tourism, thrust areas identified by the government of India for the development of infrastructure, product development and diversification, development of eco-adventure sports, cultural presentations, providing inexpensive accommodation etc. The government has also realized the importance of agro-tourism. The Planning Commission of India had constituted a Working Group for the formulation of Tenth Five Year Plan on Tourism. It has accorded high priority to tourism as an instrument of employment generation and poverty alleviation in rural and backward areas by developing the potential of agro tourism to supplement farm incomes, and heritage tourism to promote village development.

PROBLEMS OF THE AGRO-TOURISM IN SOUTH INDIA

South India has a greater potential of the development of the agro-tourism centres due to the good natural and climatic conditions. But there are some problems in the process of agro-tourism development in the state. Major challenges and problems are follows;

· Lack of perfect knowledge about the agro-tourism

· Weak communication skill and lack of commercial approach of the small farmers

· Lack of capital to develop basic infrastructure for the agro-tourism

· Ignorance of the farmers regarding to the such type of activities

· Presence of unorganized sector in the Agri-Tourism industry.

· Ensuring hygiene and basic requirements considering urban visitors

· Lakhs of farmers have small size holding, low quality land and little or no access to credit or irrigation. Have to negotiate with consistent drought. · Majority in the state are consistently drought prone

KEY TECHNIQUES FOR SUCCESS IN AGRO-TOURISM Agro-Tourism is a one of the business activities. So, farmers must have commercial mindset and some marketing techniques for the success. For the better success in the agro-tourism farmers should follow the following things; · Give a wide publicity of your tourism centre by new papers, television etc Use all possible advertisement means. · Develop contacts with the schools, colleges, NGOs, clubs, unions, organisations etc. · Train your staff or family members for reception and hospitality · understand about the customers wants and their expectations and serve 12 · Charge optimum rent and charges for the facilities/services on the commercial base · Do the artificially use local resources for the entertain / serve to tourist · Develop your website and update time to time for attract foreign tourist · Take their feedback and comments about the service and suggestions to more development and modification · Develop a good relationship with the tourist for future business and chain publicity · Develop different agro-tour packages of for different type of tourist and their expectations. · Preserve an address book and comments of the visited tourists for future tourism business · Behave sincerely with the tourists and participate with them / him · Small farmers can develop their agro-tourism centres on the basis of cooperative society.

CHAPTER FIVE

KEY TECHNIQUES FOR SUCCESS IN AGRO-TOURISM

Agro-Tourism is a one of the business activities. So, farmers must have commercial mindset and some marketing techniques for the success. For the better success in the agro-tourism farmers should follow the following things;

· Give a wide publicity of your tourism centre by new papers, television etc Use all possible advertisement means.

· Develop contacts with the schools, colleges, NGOs, clubs, unions, organisations etc.

· Train your staff or family members for reception and hospitality

· understand about the customers wants and their expectations and serve.

· Charge optimum rent and charges for the facilities/ services on the commercial base

· Do the artificially use local resources for the entertain / serve to tourist

· Develop your website and update time to time for attract foreign tourist

· Take their feedback and comments about the service and suggestions to more development and modification

· Develop a good relationship with the tourist for future business and chain publicity

· Develop different agro-tour packages of for different type of tourist and their expectations.

· Preserve an address book and comments of the visited tourists for future tourism business

· Behave sincerely with the tourists and participate with them / him · Small farmers can develop their agro-tourism centres on the basis of cooperative society.

CHAPTER SIX

CONCLUSIONS AND POLICY IMPLICATIONS

South India has a great potential to the development of agro-tourism, because of natural conditions and different types of agri products as well as variety of rural traditions, festivals. More than 45 percent of population live in the urban areas and they want enjoy rural life and to know about the rural life. It is a good opportunity to develop an agro-tourism business in South India. But there is a problem of low awareness about this business in the farmer and problem of the finance and proper view in the farmers of the South India. Hence, the agriculture departments of the districts, Agriculture Universities should try to give orientation about it and provide some innovative ideas regarding to the AgroTourism. The government should try to provide optimum financial aids to the agrotourism activities in South India by the grants and institutional finance. Bank should provide optimum financial help for the agro-tourism activities in the South India. Union of the agro-tourism service providers is also another need of these farmers which helps the agricultural tourism network in the India including South India.

References

? *Dennis M. Brown and Richard J. Reeder, 'Agri-tourism Offers Opportunities for Farm Operators'2004, U.S.A*

? *Dev, Mahendra S. (1996), Agricultural Policy Framework for Maharashtra: Issues and Options, Proceeding/Project Report No. 21, July 1996, Indira Gandhi Institute of Development Research, Mumbai.*

? *Dora Ann Hatch,(2006) Agri-tourism: A New Agricultural Business Enterprise Community Rural Development*

? *Martha Glass, North Carolina Department of Agriculture and Consumer Services 'Suggestions for helping you start an agritourism venture' November 2004*

? *Pandurang Taware ,Director Sales & Marketing, Agri Tourism Development Corporation, Pune India 'Agro-Tourism: Innovative Income Generating Activity For Enterprising Farmers'*

? *Pandurang Taware, Director – Marketing A.T.D.C., Pune, Agri – Tourism: Innovative Supplementary Income Generating Activity For Enterprising Farmers*

? *Tourism Policy of Maharashtra – 2006*

? *www.agritourism.in*

? *www.ncagr.com*

? *www.ncsla.com*

? *www.agritourismworld.com*

9 798886 293036

Printed by Libri Plureos GmbH in Hamburg,
Germany